How to Write Poetry

How to Write
POETRY

A Guided Journal with Prompts

Christopher Salerno
& Kelsea Habecker

ROCKRIDGE
PRESS

Interior and Cover Designer: Jill Lee
Art Producer: Megan Baggott
Editor: Erin Nelson
Production Editor: Ruth Sakata Corley

Illustrations © Inky Jar Design Studio/Creative Market, Nicetoseeya/Creative Market

ISBN: Print 978-1-64611-797-0

R0

To our families, with gratitude,
and to all explorers of poetry.

Other works by the authors:

Sun & Urn, by Christopher Salerno

ATM, by Christopher Salerno

Minimum Heroic, by Christopher Salerno

Whirligig, by Christopher Salerno

Hollow Out, by Kelsea Habecker

The Walrus Wives, by Kelsea Habecker

North Wife, by Kelsea Habecker

Contents

Foreword

In one of her most famous letters, Emily Dickinson said, "If I read a book and it makes my whole body so cold no fire can ever warm me, I know that is poetry." As Dickinson knew, the emotional impact of poetry can be strong. Our goal with this journal is to help you see that, while it may sometimes seem elusive or mysterious, writing poetry doesn't have to be intimidating.

Some beginning writers may have the impression that great poets pluck their poems out of thin air or, alternatively, that it takes years of studying poetry to be versed enough to write your own. While creating poetry can happen in these ways, there are also deliberate and strategic methods to draft a poem, available to everyone. After 40 collective years of teaching, we are certain there is no single correct way to write a poem. However, the best poems tend to have some characteristics in common; exploring those features and what they might open up is what this book is all about.

While you will not find exhaustive analysis in this journal, you can expect foundational information to expand your approach and energize your poems. After reading each theme, we encourage you to engage with the related prompts—to fill your journal with thoughts, fears, hopes, and musings. This book provides you with more than 100 writing exercises to get you started. What is included here comes from what we've seen spark joyful dedication in writers of all backgrounds—ages four to 84.

Anyone who has picked up this journal has the ability to write poetry. We believe that, guided by this book, you'll experience first-hand the unique ways writing poetry can encourage self-reflection, inspire a habit of artistic expression, and enrich your life. How? This kind of creative writing asks you to use descriptive imagery to enliven a moment, to consider the musical qualities of language, to reflect on relationships between similar and dissimilar things, and then to decide on the structure that best expresses your ideas, feelings, and observations. Because it is condensed, poetry offers a chance to get straight to the core of what is most important.

Ultimately, poetry is about movement. In writing a poem, we move forward in the poetic line, we move down the page, we move inward toward the self, and then back outward into the world.

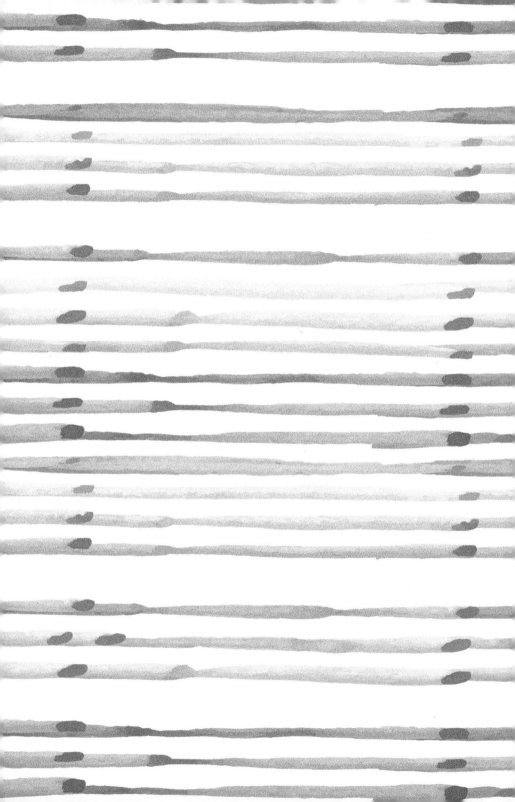

How to Use This Journal

The journal element of this book is designed to help you develop the skills, focus, imagination, and practice that poetry requires.

For each of the 26 themes, you will find:

- Theme
- Recommended reading that relates to the theme
- An excerpt of poetry that relates to the theme
- Description of the theme
- Prompts

The first 20 themes are what we'll call *tools* of the trade. These devices pertain to all creative writing. The final six themes are approaches to poetry. These are *tricks* of the trade.

All 26 themes have related prompts to stir your curiosity and deepen your practice. Themes follow a suggested path, but feel free to jump around. There is no pressure to answer every prompt; the goal is to to fill these pages as you see fit.

Finally, because reading poetry can help you write better poetry, we've made it an integral part of this journal experience. Our recommended reading showcases enduring poems, as well as contemporary work. Our hope is that you will take interest in this range of poems and allow them to inspire. All of the poems listed here can be found in their entirety online. An internet search using the poem's title should quickly reveal the poem for you to read.

ORIGINS

T. S. Eliot, "The Love Song of J. Alfred Prufrock"

Morgan Parker, "The Book of Genesis"

Kim Addonizio, "New Year's Day"

Let us go then, you and I,
When the evening is spread out against the sky

> ~T. S. Eliot, "The Love Song of
> J. Alfred Prufrock"

The creative process is mysterious. Poets find inspiration in a feeling, a single word, an image, or even a sound. Poems also come from areas of deep knowledge or skill we have developed over our lifetimes. Poetry need not come from exotic experiences. Emily Dickinson wrote extraordinary poems from her desk in a quiet New England town.

The advice to "write what you know" is important, but equally important is the ability to call upon, or explore, that which you *don't* know. A poem can offer discovery for the reader, but a poem is also an opportunity for the writer to learn something new about themselves or the world around them.

In *Letters to a Young Poet*, Rainer Maria Rilke counsels all beginners to start by "describing your sorrows and desires, the thoughts that pass through your mind and your belief in some kind of beauty... and use the things around you, the images from your dreams, and the objects that you remember." If you have been meditating on a significant truth, or on the meaning of one aspect of your life, that could become the source of a poem. Try to remain open to the many avenues of inspiration you already possess.

> Set a timer for five minutes and then write, nonstop and without judgment, starting with the phrase, "One moment I'll always remember is...." When the timer sounds, go back and add more descriptive physical details and imagery. Using whatever form you like, build a poem to share that memory with readers.

> List specific images and terminology related to something you're passionate about. When you have 20, begin writing an ode to this subject.

> Morgan Parker's poem, "The Book of Genesis" begins with the phrase, "Once I was." Write a poem that begins with the same phrase, considering your own beginnings or foundations.

IMAGERY

Elizabeth Bishop, "The Fish"

Ada Limón, "The Conditional"

Wallace Stevens, "Thirteen Ways of Looking at a Blackbird"

The apparition of these faces in the crowd:
Petals on a wet, black bow.

~Ezra Pound,
"In a Station of the Metro"

The best poems are anchored in images and some degree of action. When people say, "show don't tell," they are talking about using images to make language vivid. "Isabella went to work" tells us basic information, whereas "Isabella ran through the rain to get to work" presents a scene we can visualize.

Images resonate with readers and lend emotional and symbolic weight to a poem. As readers, we like to encounter images because they allow us to visualize the world on the page, tapping into our own memories or taking us places we've never been.

Imagery can be literal or figurative; that is, it can consist of literal, descriptive phrases, such as "his eyes were dark green;" or it may rely on something figurative, like metaphor, to create its imagery: "his eyes were a pair of dark gems." Despite the connotation of the word imagery, images need not be visual. They can involve any of the five senses. As the Romantic poet John Keats advised, "be more of an artist, and load every rift of your subject with ore," which means don't miss opportunities to use as much imagery and detail as possible.

Choose a pleasant scene from your week. Brainstorm a dozen images that come to mind from that scene. Circle those images that are most resonant for you. Describe the scene clearly enough for others to feel your joy. Rely on imagery rather than naming an emotion in the poem.

Make a list of images that convey grief. Do this again for anger, and again for love. Do they have anything in common?

Look at a poem by another poet, and circle all of the images. Now write your own new poem using those same images.

Write a poem that describes a vivid physical setting from somewhere you've traveled. Before writing, close your eyes and imagine yourself in that particular setting, focusing on specific imagery. Transport readers to that place.

METAPHOR
and SIMILE

Sylvia Plath, "Metaphors"

William Shakespeare, "Sonnet 18"

Langston Hughes, "Mother to Son"

"Hope" is the thing with feathers -
that perches in the soul -

~Emily Dickinson, "Hope Is the
Thing With Feathers"

Metaphors and similes challenge us to make new connections, to link objects or ideas that seem to have little in common; they offer new and insightful ways to see the world. We use similes and metaphors all the time to bring color and emphasis to our everyday conversations.

While a simile uses "like" or "as" to compare two things, a metaphor highlights a connection between two things. "Hope is the thing with feathers," writes Emily Dickinson. A metaphor contains two parts: the tenor, which is the subject, and the vehicle, which is the image being compared to the subject. In Dickinson's line, "hope" is the tenor; "the thing with feathers" is the vehicle.

When Shakespeare compares his lover to a summer's day, he does so by using various images of the sun, the temperature, the season, all of which carry the comparison forward. Aristotle called making metaphors a "token of genius," pointing to the challenge of creating this figure of speech. Each time we create a metaphor, we build something new out of language, like a sculpture made from words.

Open a drawer or medicine cabinet and select four different items. Using similes, write a poem to compare each of those items to some aspect of your personality.

Set a timer for three minutes and create as many definitions of "time" as you can. Put the one you're drawn to in a thought bubble and surround it with descriptive traits and images. When you have five or six traits, write a poem about "time" in which you never mention the word.

Scientists consider octopuses to be among the most fascinating creatures on earth; they have eight arms, three hearts, and no bones. Write a poem exploring possible similarities between the lives of our two species.

ENGAGING the SENSES

Fatimah Asghar, "Smell Is the Last Memory to Go"

William Stafford, "Traveling Through the Dark"

Ruth Stone, "Winter"

> *This morning I saw light kiss*
> *The silk of the roses*
> *In their second flowering*
>
> *~Stanley Kunitz, "The Round"*

"Perception is the first act of the imagination," wrote William Carlos Williams. We relate to each other and the world through our senses. While it's easy to get caught up in our thoughts and feelings, we exist in the world through our sensory experiences.

Bringing the senses into a poem can be the most potent way to breathe life into it. No matter what you're writing, try to engage as many of the physical senses—seeing, hearing, tasting, touching, and smelling—as you can. This forces you to be extra attentive to detail. After all, the universal can be found in the particular. Through the careful description of one detail, we can convey a whole universe of meaning.

Focusing on senses within a poem also keeps the poem connected to the body. Staying connected to the experiences of our bodies helps our poetry stay vital and resist becoming merely cerebral and abstract, which can feel distant and disengaging for the reader. A commitment to engaging the senses when we write keeps us tuned into the present moment of our poem.

> For each of your five senses, write down three things you are experiencing in the moment. Write a five-stanza poem in which each stanza focuses on one sense.

> Think back to a dramatic moment in your life. Jot down as many sensory memories as you can. What do you remember hearing, smelling, seeing, tasting, touching in that moment? Write the most sensory-rich paragraph or poem you can.

> Set the timer for five minutes and write about sensations you feel in your body. Is your jaw clenched, your stomach in knots? Does your heart feel open? What emotions do you notice? Where, in your body, do they reside? Write a poem that explores the relationship between emotion and body.

> Write a poem titled "Walking The Blind Dog Through The Graveyard At Dusk," and use whatever sensory detail you can imagine would be associated with that scene.

DICTION
and SYNTAX

Erin Belieu, "Love Is Not an Emergency"

Percy Bysshe Shelley, "To Night"

Thomas Sayers Ellis, "Or"

My objects dream and wear new costumes,
compelled to, it seems, by all the words in my hands
and the sea that bangs in my throat.

> *~Anne Sexton,*
> *"The Room of My Life"*

Diction is the writer's choice of words. In poetry, diction can be formal or more colloquial. The words we choose matter, especially in poetry, where there are fewer words on the page.

The power of poetry lies more in its verbs and nouns than in its adjectives. Too many adjectives add bulk and murkiness, like mixing too many paint colors and ending up with brown. The more specific a noun can be, the fewer adjectives you need to describe it. Also, try prioritizing strong, active verbs that convey motion. For instance, notice how the tone and information change when you take the sentence "I go to the bank" and replace the verb "go" with more active verbs like "run," "trudge," or even "skip."

Syntax is the order of words in a sentence. Standard English sentences usually follow a pattern of subject + verb + object. In poetry, however, parts of speech may be shifted, rearranged, or inverted to create a unique rhythm, draw emphasis to certain words, or make new connections between words.

Notice how diction differs between a love letter and an article about a medical condition. Try mixing the two by writing a poetic love letter using the diction found in a medical article.

Shakespeare's famous line, "What light from yonder window breaks?" has a more pleasing rhythm, due to its deliberate syntax, than "What light breaks from yonder window?" Shakespeare's version carries a distinct rhythm and ends by emphasizing the verb "breaks." Try writing a ten-line poem in which each line carries a distinct rhythm and ends with a verb.

LINE BREAKS

Carl Phillips, "Somewhere Holy"

Robert Creeley, "I Know a Man"

Gwendolyn Brooks, "We Real Cool"

Don, I am dying
to eat ice cream from a tray.

> ~James Wright, as recounted
> by Donald Hall in his foreword
> to James Wright's collected
> poems, Above The River.

The basic organizational structure of a poem is the line, not the sentence. In a poem, a sentence or utterance can be broken into several different lines. This allows individual parts to take on greater weight by standing out and existing on their own lines. The length of lines in a free verse poem influences rhythm, pacing, and voice. Line breaks also allow the poet to create surprise from one line to the next. In formal, metrical poetry, where the length of the line is pre-scribed by the meter, the poet will still have opportunities to create interesting lines by arranging sentences and phrases so that they begin on one line and carry over to the next.

There are two kinds of line endings: The "end-stopped line" is marked by some kind of punctuation or conclusion of a syntactic unit at the end of the line; and "enjambed line" carries a phrase over into the next line. Whether a line is end-stopped or enjambed, there will always be a natural pause at the end of the line. This allows the poet to use the final word in the line to highlight an important noun or verb, something concrete and central to the theme of the poem. It's a good rule of thumb to vary your line breaks and avoid having all end-stopped lines, which can distract the reader.

> Write a poem with only enjambed lines to describe something that involves speed. Create surprise and movement with your line breaks. How does the form fit the content?

> Rewrite a favorite poem into paragraph form. Read it aloud. How does the removal of line breaks affect the reading experience? Rewrite the poem again in lines, deciding for yourself where to break the lines. Compare it to the original.

> Try writing a poem with very short lines, then a poem with very long lines. In this instance, which do you prefer? Why? Does one more accurately represent the rhythm or flow of your own breath and these words?

> Turn this book sideways and write to the edge of the page. Now turn the page right side up and re-write the same line, breaking it into several shorter lines. How does the meaning change?

SOUNDS of POETRY

Theodore Roethke, "The Waking"

Lucie Brock-Broido, "Posthumous Seduction"

Joan Kane, "Epithalamia"

Gone, now, the baby's nurse,
a lioness who ruled the roost
and made the Mother cry.

~Robert Lowell, "Home After
Three Months Away"

Poetry was originally recited aloud and commonly accompanied by music. A first cousin to song, poetry retains musical elements, sonically engaging the ear to reinforce meaning. Regardless of whether a poem has rhyme or meter, sophisticated poets use a palette of sounds.

Four common devices poets use to enhance sonic and musical qualities include alliteration, consonance, assonance, and onomatopoeia. Alliteration is the repetition of initial consonant sounds. It can be seen in the line "six sparrows stood on spring snow." Consonance, then, is the repetition of consonant sounds within a series of words. It can be seen in the phrase "the duck ate the black cricket," where the "k" sound is repeated. Assonance, the close positioning of repeated vowel sounds, can be found in the statement, "I hear they've healed the hole in the ozone layer"—notice the repetition of "e" and "o" sounds? Lastly, onomatopoeia is the use of words that create the sounds they describe, like *buzz, clank, crash,* and *hum.*

List six words that all have the same beginning sounds and use them in a line or stanza about a recent walk around your neighborhood. Then make a list of words with similar vowel sounds and write another stanza.

Write a poem about a bird using only monosyllabic (one-syllable) words. Turn this into a poem that also mimics the sounds that bird might make.

Listen to a song performed in a language you don't speak fluently. Write down English words that come to mind as you take in the sounds. Turn this into a poem, using imagery to capture the emotional mood of the music.

Write a poem about being in the water. Use vowel sounds that recreate the sensory experience of being in water.

LYRIC IMPULSE

Walt Whitman, "Song of Myself"

Adrienne Rich, "Diving into the Wreck"

Olena Kalytiak Davis, "The Lyric 'I' Drives to Pick up Her
Children from School: A Poem in the
Post-confessional Mode"

I celebrate myself, and sing myself,
and what I assume you shall assume,
for every atom belonging to me as good belongs to you.

~Walt Whitman,
"Song of Myself"

Traditional lyric poetry is interested in the drama of human feeling (think of Sappho's passionate and often erotic lyrical poems). In contrast, longer epic poems of the past were more concerned with telling a story or conveying information (think of Homer's epic historical sagas).

Today, most of the poetry we read and write can be categorized as lyric poetry because it is generally shorter, personal, and invested in emotional expression. "Lyric" takes its name from the lyre, an instrument dating from antiquity that was often played to accompany recited poetry. While all poems contain musical qualities—such as cadence, repetition, or refrain (a repeated line or phrase)—these elements are especially important when writing poetry with lyrical intent.

When writing with a lyric impulse, the speaker in the poem usually uses the poetic "I," appearing to spontaneously utter an expression of feeling with great passion and sensuality. You might think of the lyric impulse as a poet getting swept away in a burst of emotion.

> Write a straightforward description of an activity from your day. Add sensory details and imagery. Now think of an emotional expression, like "oh, loathsome task!" or "what joy!" or "how grateful I am!" that summarizes how you feel about that activity. Turn your paragraph into a poem, repeating that expression several times in the midst of it, as a refrain.

> Write a poem that is a series of brief, passionate expressions about your favorite season.

> Create a poem with short, lyrical outbursts to express your feelings about your least favorite historical figure, sports team, movie character, or politician.

> Think of a moment where you used hushed tones to reveal a deep secret to a trusted friend. Write a poem using a lyric impulse to reveal something secret.

RHYTHM
and METER

Theodore Roethke, "My Papa's Waltz"

Edna St. Vincent Millay, "What Lips My Lips Have Kissed, and Where, and Why"

Jennifer Militello, "Lineage Is Its Own Religion"

The whiskey on your breath
Could make a small boy dizzy;
But I hung on like death:
Such waltzing was not easy.

> ~Theodore Roethke,
> "My Papa's Waltz"

Language is inherently rhythmic. As humans, we are drawn to patterned sound. Our bodies are themselves rhythmic, holding patterns in our heartbeats, breath, and brainwaves. When we speak, we stress or emphasize some syllables and leave others unstressed. This creates rhythm. Poetic meter is the deliberate arrangement of these stressed and unstressed syllables into a pattern.

To notice rhythm, listen for the stresses in the language. Can you feel the rhythm in Edna St. Vincent Millay's name, or in the title of her sonnet listed above? Notice how the stress or emphasis in the title falls on certain syllables in a repeating pattern. Millay's poem and its title use iambic pentameter, a meter with a pattern of an unstressed syllable followed by a stressed syllable.

Rhythm and meter bring music to poetry. Theodore Roethke's famous poem, "My Papa's Waltz," is a master class in rhythm; the poem itself creates music. Rhythm and meter also bring a sense of motion to poetry. Intentionally speeding up the rhythm of our words in certain sections of the poem can add a sense of urgency or intensity; slowing down the rhythm has a quieting effect.

> With rhythm in mind, write a poem that conveys something frantic. Then write a poem that conveys something relaxed. Use line breaks to help you achieve a faster or slower rhythm. Use sensory detail and imagery where you can.

> Create lines that each mimic the rhythm of a heartbeat or your breath. Use these lines in a poem that expresses your feelings to someone important to you.

> Write a poem that delivers good news to someone you love. Experiment with rhythm to see how it feels to deliver that news at a fast pace, in a burst of energy, versus drawing out the message to deliver it more slowly and with dramatic suspense.

> Try writing a poem that uses iambic pentameter as its meter. To take it further, you could write a full sonnet, which is 14 lines of iambic pentameter.

_____

_____

_____

_____

_____

_____

_____

_____

_____

_____

_____

_____

_____

_____

_____

_____

_____

_____

_____

_____

RHYME

A. E. Stallings, "Sea Girls"

W. H. Auden, "Funeral Blues"

Marianne Moore, "To A Steamroller"

*In sober mornings do not thou rehearse
the holy incantation of a verse?*

~Robert Herrick, "When He
Would Have His Verses Read"

Humans appreciate the sound of rhyming. When poetry was primarily an oral tradition, rhyme made poems easier to memorize so they could be shared. Rhyme has persisted in poetry for centuries. In the 20th century, when some poets felt constrained by it, they began to also write unrhymed poetry. Despite the freedom today's poets experience in their approach, rhyming is still very much alive.

There are several different types of rhyming that can inform your poetry. Perfect rhyme is when two words rhyme exactly, such as "storm" and "form." Near rhyme is when two words *nearly* rhyme, such as "fear" and "fire." Internal rhyme is when a rhyme happens *within* the line instead of at the end, for instance, "The stormed formed waves." Both near rhyme and internal rhyme add subtle texture, interest, and music to poetry. Contemporary examples of these devices can be found in hip-hop or rap music.

Poets often use stanzas to establish a rhyme scheme—a pattern of end rhyme. The poet chooses what rhyme scheme to follow, for example AA, then selects words to adhere to the structure. You can experiment with various patterns and degrees of rhyme, all of which will present you with an exciting challenge.

List 10 near-rhymes for the word "storm." See if you can use all of them in one poem about a memory of a storm.

Think of a favorite nursery rhyme. Using the same rhyme scheme, rewrite it, giving it a message that applies to adults rather than children.

Listen to a few hip hop songs; pay attention to their rhyme scheme. Take note when you hear end, internal, and near rhyme. What effect does it have on the message of the song? Write a verse using these techniques.

TONE

Ross Gay, "The Opera Singer"

Patricia Lockwood, "The Hypno-Domme Speaks, and Speaks
and Speaks"

James Tate, "The List of Famous Hats"

Wild nights - Wild nights!
Were I with thee
Wild nights should be
Our luxury!

~Emily Dickinson,
"Wild Nights"

Tone is the mood of the poem, its emotional complexity. Much contemporary poetry is personal and intimate in tone, capable of expressing a range of emotion. Poems can be fearful, angry, longing, erotic, grieving, playful, humorous, ironic, regretful—the list goes on.

Tone is also the attitude of the speaker toward their subject. In speech, we convey tone through inflections and emphasis. In poetry writing, however, tone is expressed through our choice of words, images, rhythms, punctuation, and line breaks.

A poem with a consistent tone can be satisfying because of its sustained emotion. Or, a poem's tone can change to convey the shifting mood of the narrator. Changing tone at the end of the poem is a common technique used to create heightened emotional impact, and some traditional forms, like sonnets or haikus, often have tone changes in their final lines.

> Write a paragraph describing an authority figure in your life. Break those sentences into lines to create a poem with an admiring tone toward your subject. Now, do the exercise again but use different line breaks to write a poem with a suspicious tone.

> Write two poems about an impending winter storm. In the first, imagine welcoming winter; let your poem's language convey a reverent tone. In the second, imagine you despise wintry weather. Notice how your diction shifts the tone.

> Create a poem with a sleepy mood by using long sentences and long vowel sounds. Now write a second poem that has the opposite effect, making the reader alert and wide-eyed.

> Write a poem that begins with a neutral statement, like "It's fine," and then explore different tonal interpretations of that statement throughout your poem. Consider sarcasm as a tonal device.

PERSONA

Natasha Trethewey, "Letter Home"

Amy Gerstler, "Siren"

Claudia Cortese, "The Birds Inside Her"

I is another.

> *~Arthur Rimbaud,*
> *"I is another" (statement*
> *written in a letter)*

Not all poems are autobiographical. As poets, we sometimes inhabit other identities who may say something we don't wish to (or wouldn't dare) say as ourselves. This person, or "persona," is an alternate voice who narrates the poem. It can be a movie star, a fictional character, your childhood doll, or any personality you want to embody.

Persona allows us to explore tensions in our own lives, and more deeply examine things outside of ourselves. Persona grants us the ability to write about difficult subjects with greater freedom by adopting the voice of someone or something else rather than relying on variations in our own voice. It may seem paradoxical, but we must not presume that the words spoken in a poem are from the perspective of the poet. Instead, we recognize the creative freedom poetry allows.

Before writing, consider incorporating research into your persona poem to make the voice as convincing as possible. If your persona is a well-known figure, learn about that person and carefully choose your details, diction, and voice so that the poem truly embodies the persona you desire.

Choose a poem you've written in this journal and rewrite it in the voice of a character from your favorite movie or novel. What do they have to say about the subject? How are you using line breaks, diction, and imagery to differentiate this character?

Write a poem to yourself from the perspective of your desk chair, which you sit on every day. (You could also try your favorite pair of shoes, or your coffee mug.) Use sensory detail.

Think of an animal in your life and write a poem from the perspective of that animal. What do you think it might want to say about life with you?

STYLE and VOICE

Rosebud Ben-Oni, "Poet Wrestling with Her Empire of Dirt"

Kaveh Akbar, "Pilgrim Bell"

Monica Youn, "Self-Portrait in a Wire Jacket"

my father moved through dooms of love
through sames of am through haves of give,
singing each morning out of each night
my father moved through depths of height

> ~e e cummings, "my father
> moved through dooms of love"

Poet and philosopher Samuel Taylor Coleridge described poetry as "the best words in the best order." But how does one know which words are best, and in which order to put them? How can so many great poems be so wildly different from each other? It's often a matter of style. Some poets have a style that incorporates a lot of punctuation, while others don't use it at all. Some rely more heavily on rhythm, some less. These are all aspects of style.

Think of a poem's style as a layer of clothing it wears on top of its deeper themes. Figures of speech, grammar, syntax (the order of words), rhythm, line breaks—as well as all other poetic devices—can work together to create style. Push any one of these elements beyond normal levels and you can create stylistic interest in a poem.

Similar to style, you can think of voice as an expression of self on the page. Voice is the presence of the poet, or their persona, in the poem. When you arrange your lines to capture a certain manner of speech, when you consider the amount of white space you leave between lines, or when you find a suitable rhythm for the speaker of the poem, you are conveying voice. The more you write, the more you will develop your own voice and style that will evolve as you do.

> Write a poem that is all one, long sentence about a moment of extreme frustration. Don't use punctuation. Use your line breaks to create moments of pause in the poem.

> Write a poem that asks at least five questions, regardless of the subject of the poem. Let each of these questions stand alone on its own line.

> What do you tend to do naturally in your writing? Do you use a lot of figurative imagery, repetition, or rhyme? Write a poem with a wildly different approach from your typical style. To go deeper with this, experiment with your syntax.

FIRST and LAST LINES

James Wright, "Lying in a Hammock at William Duffy's Farm in Pine Island, Minnesota"

torrin a. greathouse, "Aubade Beginning in Handcuffs"

Anne Sexton, "Her Kind"

I lean back, as the evening darkens and comes on.
A chicken hawk floats over, looking for home.
I have wasted my life.

~James Wright "Lying In A
Hammock at William Duffy's
Farm in Pine Island, Minnesota"

Two areas of prime real estate exist in a poem, especially in free verse poetry where the writer has many choices regarding where to break lines. One of these prime areas is the first line of the poem. The opening line sets the tone, establishes voice, and grabs the reader's attention. The goal is to make a first line compel the reader to want to read further, like when Anne Sexton starts her poem by boldly declaring "I have gone out, a possessed witch." Strong first lines often make a bold claim or revelation.

The last line of the poem is equally important. A last line can reveal a catharsis or open up a new perspective for consideration. Poet Stanley Kunitz gave the advice to "end on an image and don't explain it." This suggests leaving readers with something sensory, a detail that will resonate in their minds. As the poet Donald Hall once said, "a poem should either close the lid on the box or open it up to the horizon."

> Brainstorm a dozen startling or dramatic phrases. Choose one you think will hook readers and write a poem with that phrase as your first line. (Remember to engage the senses.)

> Often, poets use the last line of the poem to deliver an emotional jab or share an epiphany. Use sensory detail to write a poem about your hometown. Let your final line be a dramatic, insightful, or cathartic expression about home.

> Write about a recent experience in your life where the beginning was an ending and the end was a beginning. Use metaphor as you do this. Turn this into a poem with the same first and last line.

NARRATIVE IMPULSE

Stephen Dobyns, "Tomatoes"

Natalie Diáz, "It Was the Animals"

Denise Duhamel, "The Threat"

Then it is autumn in the body.
Your hands are cold.
Then it is winter and we are still at war.

~Kevin Prufer,
"In a Beautiful Country"

While lyric poems primarily feature self-expression, narrative poems are concerned with telling a story. Some of the greatest works of epic poetry fall into this narrative category, including *Beowulf* and Homer's *Odyssey*. A more contemporary, famous example of a narrative poem is Edgar Allan Poe's "The Raven."

Yet, a narrative poem doesn't have to tell a story that is a big, epic saga. It can simply narrate an everyday event that the poet wants to consider more deeply. Open to a range of poetic techniques such as meter or rhyme, the narrative poem may include action and dialogue. Similar to a novel or a short story, a narrative poem may have plot, a chronology of events, setting, and characters, too.

Traditional forms of narrative poetry include epics, ballads, and even entire novels written in verse. If you've got a specific story you want to recount, the narrative form of poetry might be the best approach.

> Write a poem about a recent incident as if you were telling a story to a room full of people. Incorporate a conversational tone and dialogue.

> Write a paragraph about a frightening experience. Provide specific details to describe the incident step-by-step, allowing the reader to experience the fright. Now, take that paragraph and break it into lines, creating even more suspense with enjambed line breaks.

> Use a current news headline as your poem title. Craft a poem that describes the event and its impact. Use words from the news article. To take this further, use metaphor to link this event with a larger theme.

REPETITION

Jane Kenyon, "Otherwise"

Joy Harjo, "Everybody Has A Heartache: A Blues"

Jennifer Bartlett, "Autobiography/Anti-Autobiography"

What you can't hear is the light caught inside each bud.
What you can't hear is the leaves caught inside each spark.

> *~Nick Flynn,*
> *"What You Can't Hear"*

Repetition is a powerful tool for poets to emphasize meaningful language. Poets rely on repetition to bring a poem to life by creating a sense of rhythm and urgency. Some formal poems use a refrain or a repeating line in their form. The repeated language in these poems can establish or accentuate a theme, or create an echo for a strong sentiment.

One technique for developing memorable repetition is through parallelism. Parallelism, shown in the above example by Nick Flynn, occurs when a poet constructs grammatically similar lines, repeating a specific word, phrase, or idea. This creates continuity between the ideas and emphasizes the importance of the language. Anaphora, a specific type of parallelism with roots in biblical Psalms, emphasizes repeating words at the beginning of each line of the poem.

Chants at protests or political rallies rely on key words repeated over and over again. Write a poem that uses a word or phrase repeatedly, like a chant, to convey an important idea or motif in the poem.

Write an anaphora poem, in which each line of the poem begins with the same phrase, like "I now know..." or "The morning reveals...."

Think of a phrase that was repeated in your childhood by a parent or a teacher. Write a poem in which that line appears in every stanza, and let each stanza explore how that phrase impacted you in different ways throughout your life.

PERSONIFICATION

Ada Limón, "Downhearted"

Emily Dickinson, "Because I Could Not Stop for Death"

Charles Simic, "Eyes Fastened with Pins"

O rose, thou art sick!

~William Blake,
"The Sick Rose"

For centuries, poets have humanized objects, animals, deities, and states of being. They do this by endowing them with what makes us human: love, joy, anger, sadness—even death. Romantic poets, for instance, often personify different elements of nature to explore their intense communion with the natural world.

Personification is a way for the poet to take an abstract concept and discuss it artfully, using specific details and sensory language. Through this tactic, the poet infuses character into what was before an inanimate object or abstract idea. When Emily Dickinson creates a scenario whereby the narrator is courted by Death, she endows Death with kindness and even presents him as a chivalrous character, a suitor who kindly stops his carriage for her before they ride off together into immortality.

Personification is one of many figures of speech that, like metaphor or simile, allows the poet to build broader and more striking connections between elements of the world. Different from persona, an alternate identity a poet assumes throughout a poem, personification is a device a poet can bring into any poem at any time.

> Personify Fear or Grief as a character who has decided to visit for the weekend. Write a narrative poem detailing your time together.

> Write a poem personifying your hands or eyes. What kind of life might they lead if you would only release them into the wild? Metaphor will be useful in this poem.

> Create a poem personifying an item of clothing in your closet. What kind of temperament does this piece of clothing have? What are its preferences or tastes? Try exploring repetition in this poem.

TRUTH and LIES

Robert Lowell, "Skunk Hour"

Maggie Smith, "Good Bones"

Danielle Pafunda, "The Dead Girls Speak in Unison"

> *Out of the ash*
> *I rise with my red hair*
> *And I eat men like air.*
>
> ~Sylvia Plath, "Lady Lazarus"

Some people presume poetry is more nonfiction than fiction, insisting that poems remain aligned with literal fact, perhaps from autobiographical details or observations reported by a persona. Indeed, long before obsession with reality TV, confessional poets of the mid-twentieth century relied heavily on details from their own lives and their intimate relationships to craft poems. These poems can be compelling in their candid honesty.

Other poets recognize that truth can be much bigger than a list of facts, drawing instead on the imaginative freedom of fiction. Many poets invent details for the sake of the poem's sound, rhythm, color, or tone. Poet Richard Hugo writes in the book *The Triggering Town*, "A good teacher can save a young poet years by simply telling him things he need not waste his time on, like trying to remain true to the facts." Put another way, poet Dean Young says, "The blood's always fake, but you've got to try to make the bleeding look real."

> Write a poem comprised almost entirely of lies about yourself. Somewhere in the poem, reveal one important truth about who you are or something that matters to you greatly. Focus on using alliteration, assonance, or consonance to enhance the music of your poem.

> Write a poem about the little daily lies you tell about yourself or the world.

> Reflect on a time when you lied to protect yourself from a truth you weren't ready to face. Brainstorm a list of emotions that captured how you felt when you relied on the lie. Now, write a poem that reflects the letting go of these emotions.

SURREALISM

Dean Young, "Thrown as If Fierce and Wild"

Heather Christle, "The Tooth"

Sabrina Orah Mark, "The Very Nervous Family"

My wife with hair of a wood fire
with the thoughts of heat lightning
with the waist of an hourglass
with the waist of an otter in the teeth of a tiger

~Andre Breton, "Free Love"

Surrealism invites the unexpected into our consciousness. As such, Surrealist poetry is famous for its unusual imagery and diction. Surrealism emerged in 1920s Paris, then spread around the world. Many surrealist poets were inspired by the psychoanalysis of Sigmund Freud and Carl Jung, with its emphasis on dreams and unconscious thought. Still a popular practice in contemporary poetry today, Surrealist poetry taps into the old wells of the mind, and often moves beyond reasonable language and logic to find deeper truths.

To develop unusual imagery, try to find a relationship between two very dissimilar things. Do not hesitate when describing the strange links between them as you write. Surrealist poetry is about moving forward without constraints. When we take risks as poets, we create surprise for the reader. As the poet Mary Ruefle says,

"One of the loveliest possibilities is that the truth is made of glass but shaped like a hammer."

> Find an unusual or uncommon word in the dictionary, but do not read the definition. Use the word as the title of a poem; write a poem that creates your own definition and history of the word.

> Write a poem based on a strange dream you've had. Include the bizarre details of the dream, no matter how nonsensical they might be. Use metaphor and imagery to make the poem clear to readers who didn't experience the dream. (If you can't remember a recent dream, unleash your creativity and make one up.)

> Think of a moment when you experienced strong emotion. Describe that moment literally, then use surreal details to shock readers into understanding the intensity of your emotional experience.

IMITATION

Robert Frost, "The Road Not Taken"

Ai, "Conversation"

Mary Oliver, "Wild Geese"

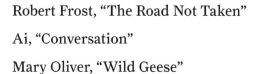

What did I know
thinking myself
able to go
alone all the way.

~*Robert Creeley,*
"Love Comes Quietly"

We grow as poets as much by reading as by writing. When you assume the voice, style, and form of another poet you are able to feel what it is like to inhabit that writer's frame of mind, hopefully learning something about your own writing process. Imitation, in this case, can be the first step toward discovery and growth.

When considering a poem that you want to imitate, first ask yourself what you notice about the poem's shape on the page. Has the poet used long or short lines? Has the poet used mostly multisyllabic words, or shorter, monosyllabic words? Are there metaphors or other figurative language? Poems with distinct features like a consistent meter, a repeated refrain, a dominant central metaphor, or a strong tone can be fun to imitate, and this can push you to try what you might not ordinarily attempt in your own poems.

If you borrow anything of substance from the original, it is a good idea to credit the author by name either in your poem's title or else in a short statement between the title and the first line of the poem.

> Choose any poem you like; list its verbs and the dominant poetic techniques employed by the poet. Craft your own poem in a similar style, but about a different subject. Title your poem, "Variation On A Theme By _____."

> Imitate a poem that you don't like, or a poem with a radically different style from your own. If you use punctuation in your poems, choose a poem that doesn't use any. If you write short lines, choose a poem with long lines. If you write long poems, choose a short poem.

> Think of a favorite poem. Following that poet's style, write a sequel for the original poem.

POETRY of PROTEST

Evie Shockley, "anti-immigration"

Carmen Giménez Smith, "Decoy Gang War Victim"

Kevin Young, "Nightstick [A Mural for Michael Brown]"

Francisco X. Alarcón, "'Mexican' Is Not a Noun"

What is poetry which does not save Nations or people?

~Czeslaw Milosz, "Dedication"

Poetry has long been a vehicle for resistance. Throughout history, poets have often been imprisoned for highlighting injustices and rallying communities to take action. Because poems carry the unique ability to crystalize and amplify the messages of the most oppressed among us during times of crisis, poets continue to use their verses to speak truth to power.

A good protest poem has the power to inspire and transform those who read it. Audre Lorde once wrote, "Poetry is not a luxury. It is a vital necessity of our existence. It forms the quality of the light within which we predicate our hopes and dreams toward survival and change...." Protest poems can carry a tone of compassion, confrontation, reverence, even fear. Many argue the mere writing of poetry in the face of injustice is itself an act of protest, whether in our homes, communities, or larger world.

> Make a list of issues that you feel strongly enough about to make a public demonstration. Are there common themes? Write a protest poem about one of them, using rhetorical questions. (Consider sending it to an elected representative.)

> Write a manifesto for yourself, a statement that expresses who you are, what matters most to you, or how you feel the world should operate. What are lines you can't cross within yourself? Find a repeating refrain to use as your rallying call.

> Write a poem in which alternating stanzas depict two different sides of a divisive issue.

> Write a protest poem to a loved one protesting an everyday activity they do that irritates you. Are there elements of a political struggle in this personal protest?

POETRY of PLACE

Frank O'Hara, "The Day Lady Died"

Eduardo C. Corral, "In Colorado My Father Scoured and Stacked Dishes"

Tracy K. Smith, "The United States Welcomes You"

I placed a jar in Tennessee,
And round it was, upon a hill.
It made the slovenly wilderness
Surround that hill.

> ~Wallace Stevens,
> "Anecdote of the Jar"

Poet Wendell Berry once said, "If you don't know where you are, you don't know who you are." Writing about a place is an opportunity to evoke the character of a location using your unique perspective. To capture the spirit of a place, a poet must rely on heightened imagery and sensory detail, on observation and insight.

In the Romantic tradition, poems about place were often used to commune with nature, exploring themes of love and loss. Poems about place do not always celebrate; any place offers both comfort and challenge. Many poems about place focus on how humans have an ever-changing and even difficult relationship with their environment.

The best poems of place make use of a location to communicate feelings shared by readers who have also thought about where they come from, where they live, or what it means to be home (or home-less). Poetry of place may be unique to one person in one location, but it can also address universal themes. After all, a poem about a place is also a poem about the nature of our experience in the world.

Imagine standing in front of a vast landscape or dramatic feature in the natural world—like the Grand Canyon, a glacier, or the ocean. Brainstorm a list of imagery that communicates the sense of awe you feel in that place; use as many of those words as you can in a poem.

Think of a city you love. Using details to engage the senses, write a poem that shows how it is unique from other cities and why it is your favorite.

Write a poem about a favorite room from your childhood home, using specific details and sensory references to evoke a clear sense of place.

Where, outside, have you felt most alive? Reflect on that experience, using refrain.

EKPHRASTIC POETRY

Diane Seuss, "Still Life with Two Dead Peacocks and a Girl"

W. H. Auden, "Musee des Beaux Arts"

Victoria Chang, "Edward Hopper Study: Hotel Room"

Yet it is less the horror than the grace
which turns the gazer's spirit into stone

> ~Percy Bysshe Shelley, "On the
> Medusa of Leonardo da Vinci
> in the Florentine Gallery"

Ekphrastic poetry responds to art. While the connection between poetry and music is natural due to their shared lyricism, there is also a strong connection between poetry and visual art. Many poets are drawn to writing about art because of the mutual reliance on symbols, imagery, emotional intensity, and ability to evocatively portray a moment in time. Homer, the blind author of the great epic poem *The Iliad*, wrote some of the earliest known ekphrastic passages, most notably a detailed description of the shield of Achilles. Romantic poets like Keats would later write ekphrastic poetry to express the personal impact of a particularly beautiful piece of art.

Ekphrastic poets rely on many different methods. Some ekphrastic poems analyze and respond to the artwork, while others invent or explore possible narratives behind it. Ekphrastic poems can also function as direct addresses to the artist or subject of the original piece, allowing the poet to inhabit its world.

> Ask a question to a piece of art. Use this question as your first line, then let the rest of the poem answer the question, from the perspective of the art itself or the artist who made it.

> Think of a moment when you were deeply moved by a work of art. What about the piece moved you? Explore your feelings through a poem; to go deeper, try a formal poem such as a sestina or a sonnet.

> Imagine your favorite piece of art has been destroyed. Your poem will be the only record of it. Use as many specific and sensory details as possible so that the meaning, power, and visual intensity of the art comes to life in your poem.

OBJECT POETRY

Rainer Maria Rilke, "Archaic Torso Of Apollo"

May Swenson, "A Navajo Blanket"

Robert Bly, "Looking at a Dead Wren In My Hand"

Onion,
luminous flask,
your beauty formed
petal by petal

~Pablo Neruda,
"Ode to the Onion"

Poetry can allow us to examine familiar things in fresh ways. When we consider objects outside of their usual environments, we begin to notice new insight. Historically, an object poem takes a descriptive look at an inanimate object, building on any significance or connection between it and the human world. By focusing intently on an object's qualities, features, physical form, and functions, a poet may inevitably discover the object's symbolic ability to reveal something profound.

Consider the shape of a teapot. What about its function carries some connection or similarity to your own body, your own life? How might you relate to, personify, or compare yourself to this object? What differences are there between you and the object both literally and metaphorically? Does this object have a history, real or imagined? When writing object poetry, begin by describing your chosen object in a non-prejudiced way, and then allow any larger truths or ideas to build from those details.

> Imagine aliens have visited earth. What item would they find that baffles them most? Write a poem from the persona of an alien who is trying to understand this mysterious object.

> Look around your kitchen; choose a common item such as a spoon, bowl, a piece of fruit. How does the object relate to someone close to you? How does it relate to a well-known fairy tale? How does it relate to your ideas about faith or religion?

> Go on a walk and discover a natural object, like a rock or an acorn. Write a brief scientific description of the object. Then, ask the object a list of 10 questions. Using descriptions, sonic elements like alliteration, and the questions, write a poem that explores the object as if it were conveying a message to you.

OCCASIONAL POETRY

Matthew Zapruder, "Graduation Day"

Louise Gluck, "Epithalamium"

Li-Young Lee, "Little Father"

Say it plain: that many have died for this day.
Sing the names of the dead who brought us here,
who laid the train tracks, raised the bridges

~Elizabeth Alexander,
"Praise Song For The Day"

An occasional poem is one written in response to an occasion, such as a birthday, a wedding, a victory, a major event, or a death, and is often intended for a public reading. Occasional poetry has been a significant form of expression throughout history, including in ancient Greece and Rome. Billy Collins, U.S. poet laureate at the time of the 9/11 attacks, wrote a poem, "The Names," in honor of the victims. He read the poem before a special joint session of Congress held in New York City. Elizabeth Alexander wrote and performed "Praise Song for the Day" for President Barack Obama's inauguration in 2009.

The occasional poem includes several popular genres, including epithalamia (wedding poems), dirges or elegies (funerary poems), odes, and many others. The German poet Johann Wolfgang von Goethe deemed occasional poetry "the highest kind" because of the role it can play in lending meaning and significance to the events of public life. Occasional poems can be highly personal or more objective. They may focus on meaningful symbolism or other universal characteristics of the occasion. The occasional poem uses an individual event to comment on the broader trajectories of our lives.

> Think of a major ceremonial event from your past, like a wedding, graduation, birth, or funeral. Write a poem that could have been read at the event, but write from an outside perspective—as someone observing the event—not from your own perspective as a participant in the event. Sensory details will help you capture the moment.

> Write a poem to commemorate an exciting but less ceremonial event, such as a job promotion, a move to a new place, or the acquisition of a new car.

> Write an elegy, but let it commemorate the loss of something ordinary and small, like a missing key or an hour lost in a doctor's waiting room. Use specific details to convey the loss to readers.

FOUND POETRY

Terrance Hayes, "The Golden Shovel"

David Lehman, "Oxford Cento"

Catherine Pierce, "High Dangerous"

Mary Ruefle, "From A Little White Shadow"

The fragments I have shored against my ruins.

~T. S. Eliot, "The Wasteland"

Hyper-attuned to language, poets learn to find inspiration in unexpected places. This is most literally demonstrated in found poetry. Found poetry takes words, phrases, or even whole sentences from other sources—such as menus, signs, pamphlets, or owner's manuals—and rearranges them into poems. Repurposing language taken from one context and arranging it in a new setting can offer the poet fresh insight, irony, humor, or simply a fun and creative exercise.

In 1920, the rebellious poet Tristan Tzara created a method of writing a poem by using random words he pulled one at a time from a bag. The resulting poem was initially nonsensical, but its juxtaposition of words fueled his creativity and offered a starting place for new work. Another type of found poem is the cento, a poem comprised of single lines taken from various other sources in order to form a new poem.

An erasure or redacted poem is another type of found poem that involves erasing or redacting carefully selected words from a page of printed text to reveal a new poem in the text that remains. This can be a dynamic exercise because as poets chisel away at a block of text, much like a sculptor, they find a new and interesting figure remaining.

Find an instruction manual for a piece of technology in your home. Choose samples of language from it to create a poem that functions as an instruction manual for how to make an important decision.

Look for interesting language in spam email. Compile these examples of found language into a letter poem (an epistolary poem).

Recipes and cookbooks are rich sources of interesting language. Take a favorite recipe and re-purpose the language into a poem that speaks to an issue larger than cooking, such as family or community.

Conduct an internet search using an anatomical word, such as "muscle" or "ear canal." Print out an article or the search results to create an erasure poem that reveals something about you.

Common Poetic Terms

ALLITERATION: The repetition of initial consonant sounds in a line of poetry.

ASSONANCE: The close positioning of repeated vowel sounds in a poem.

CONSONANCE: The repetition of consonant sounds within a series of words.

COUPLET: A two-line stanza.

END-STOPPED LINE: A line that is marked by some kind of punctuation or conclusion of a syntactic unit at the end of the line.

ENJAMBMENT: The continuation of a sentence or phrase from one poetic line to the next.

FIGURATIVE LANGUAGE: Language that goes beyond literal description to create more interesting, colorful, or comparative language.

IAMBIC PENTAMETER: The most commonly used type of meter in poetry, iambic pentameter creates a pattern of an unstressed (unaccented) syllable followed by a stressed (accented) syllable. This pattern is repeated a total of five times in each line of the poem, amounting to ten syllables in each line. For example: "At **nine** the **ris**en **moon** was **all** a**glow**."

METER: A deliberately recurring pattern of unstressed (unaccented) and stressed (accented) syllables.

MOTIF: An image or idea repeated throughout a poem.

QUATRAIN: A four-line stanza.

REFRAIN: A repeating line or phrase used throughout a poem.

RHYTHM: The beat of the poem (the rise and fall of unstressed and stressed syllables) regardless of meter or form.

STANZA: The word stanza is an Italian word meaning "room." A stanza is a group of lines that can form the basic structural unit within a poem. The choice of which type of stanza a poem employs impacts the rhythm and style of a poem. For example, poems that wish to provide more room for pause and reflection within the poem might be written in shorter stanzas and allow for more white space on the page. Rhyme scheme, if used, can also impact the choice of stanza type.

TERCET: A three-line stanza.

Revisiting Your Work

Revision means to look at again, and revising is one of the most important activities for a writer. The point of revision is to look closely at your poem and reconsider the choices you've made.

Revision is not solely about identifying areas that are less strong. It is also a continuation of the curiosity and exploration you desired when you set out to write in the first place.

Here are a few techniques to guide you:

> Put the poem away for a few hours, even a few days, so that you can return to it with a fresh perspective. Returning, you will be struck by areas that lack clarity or precision.

> Rewrite your draft into a paragraph. This paragraph will be more accessible to you as you revise. It will allow you to tinker with the poem's logic, meanings, narrative, rhythm, and punctuation more easily. Return your draft to poem form afterward. This is a good moment to consider what form or shape you want your poem to have.

> Look at your poem's beginning and ending. Does the poem need to be cropped, like a photo, to bring the heart of the matter into focus? Often, early draft opening lines are warm-up, and the more interesting lines don't occur until later in the poem; the warm-up lines can be cut. Consider, too, if you have written past your best ending, perhaps in an unnecessary attempt to explain the poem.

> Look closely at line breaks. Are yours deliberate? Consider how the poem looks on the page. You can alter the shape,

rhythm, or pacing of the poem through your line breaks or word choice.

Focus especially on places where you are telling readers something you could be showing more clearly with imagery or metaphor.

Consider whether you are relying on clichés. A cliché is an expression that has been overused to the extent that it loses its original meaning or impact. It may have once imparted wisdom, but now it has been used or said so often that it doesn't carry the weight it once did. As poets, one of our goals is to make writing so sharp and original that it, too, becomes a cliché used by people years from now to talk about the ins and outs of their own lives.

Grow your skills by joining a writing group or participating in poetry readings. This will bring you into direct contact with others' poetry and help you gain more clarity about your work.

Where to Submit Your Work

While this is not an exhaustive list of publishing venues for poetry, it represents a selection of journals that we admire and recommend.

Able Muse, a journal of poetry, fiction, and nonfiction, with a focus on metrical poetry. Submissions accepted all year.
>> https://www.ablemuse.com

Acorn, a journal of haikus. Submissions read during January/February and July/August for publication in April and October.
>> https://acornhaiku.com/submissions/

Adroit, a journal of poetry and prose, publishing work by new and established writers. Submissions read during fall and spring.
>> https://theadroitjournal.org

Alaska Quarterly Review, a journal of poetry, fiction, and nonfiction publishing both new and established writers. Submissions read from October to December, and February to March.
>> https://aqreview.org/writers-guidelines/

Albion Review, a journal of poetry, fiction, and nonfiction publishing work by college undergraduate writers. Each submission is eligible for a $200 prize. Submissions accepted in the month of October for publication in spring of the following year.
>> https://albionreview.com

Chestnut Review, a poetry, fiction, and nonfiction journal with an emphasis on narrative. Submissions accepted year-round.
>> https://chestnutreview.com

Firewords Quarterly, an independent literary magazine in the UK with a strong emphasis on new writers. They publish theme issues, and they accept poetry, fiction, and nonfiction. Submissions accepted in spring and fall.
>> https://firewords.co.uk

Green Mountains Review publishes poetry, fiction, essays, and book reviews. The editors are open to a wide range of styles and subject matter, and are also always looking for work that pushes the boundaries. Submissions accepted from September 1 to March 1.
>> http://greenmountainsreview.com/

North American Review is the oldest literary magazine in America (founded in 1815) and one of the most respected. They are interested in quality poetry, fiction, and nonfiction on any subject. Submissions accepted all year.
>> https://northamericanreview.org

Palette Poetry publishes emerging and established poets, no matter the style. Submissions accepted year-round.
>> http://www.palettepoetry.com

Poetry Magazine is the oldest and most prestigious monthly magazine devoted to verse in the English-speaking world. Submissions accepted all year.
>> https://www.poetryfoundation.org/poetrymagazine

Prairie Schooner publishes stories, poems, interviews, imaginative essays of general interest, and reviews of current books of poetry and fiction. Submissions accepted from September 1 to May 1.
>> https://prairieschooner.unl.edu

Rattle is a poetry-only magazine publishing all styles: formal poems, epic poems, lyric poems, narrative poems, surreal poems, prose poems, visual poems, etc. It maintains a Poets Respond page online, which publishes political poems weekly. Submissions accepted all year.
>> http://www.rattle.com

Salt Hill is an eclectic journal known for publishing new and emerging poets. They accept submissions for the Philip Booth Poetry Award between May 15 and August 1. Submissions accepted from July 1 through September 30, and January 1 through March 31.
>> http://salthilljournal.org/

Sycamore Review is Purdue University's internationally acclaimed literary journal, publishing poetry, fiction, and nonfiction by new and established writers. Submissions accepted from Aug 1 to Mar 31.
>> http://www.sycamorereview.com

The Journal publishes quality poetry by both emerging and established authors. Submissions are accepted year-round.
>> http://thejournalmag.org/

Thrush is an online journal of poetry that appears six times a year, showcasing the best work received throughout the calendar year. Submissions are accepted on a rolling basis.
>> http://www.thrushpoetryjournal.com

Tupelo Quarterly publishes poetry by emerging and established writers and artists of many sensibilities and styles. It also invites submissions every year for the Poetry Open Prize, which is judged by a prominent poet. Submissions accepted in spring and fall.
>> http://www.tupeloquarterly.com

Valparaiso Poetry Review publishes poems, book reviews, author interviews, and essays about poetry or poetics from well-known and emerging poets. Submissions accepted all year.

>> https://www.valpo.edu/vpr

Waxwing is a literary journal promoting the tremendous cultural diversity of contemporary American literature, with a stated mission of including poets of all cultural identities. Submissions accepted from August 1 to May 31.

>> http://www.waxwingmag.org

A Poetry Library

A Poetry Handbook, by Mary Oliver: A book that offers common-sense advice on the fundamentals of writing poetry by Pulitzer Prize winner Mary Oliver.

Asian American Voices in Poetry, by The Poetry Foundation: An online collection of poetry and articles exploring traditional and contemporary Asian American culture.

Beauty is a Verb, edited by Sheila Black, Jennifer Bartlett, and Michael Northen: An anthology of poetry, essays, and writings on disability and poetry.

Best Words Best Order, by Steven Dobyns: A book that explores the mystery of how the poet's work communicates thoughts and feelings between writer and reader.

Celebrating Black History Month, by The Poetry Foundation: A collection of both traditional and contemporary poems, articles, and podcasts that explore African American history and culture.

Don't Read Poetry, by Stephanie Burt: A book offering an accessible introduction to the task of reading, comprehending, and appreciating modern and contemporary poetry.

LGBTQ Pride Poems, by The Poetry Foundation: A collection of poetry and articles exploring traditional and contemporary LGBTQ poetry.

Madness, Rack, and Honey, by Mary Ruefle: A book of collected lectures on poetry writing from one of the most inventive and provocative contemporary poets writing today.

On Difficulty in Poetry, by Reginald Shepherd: An essay outlining several different types of poetic difficulty; helps diffuse some of the inhibitions readers have about the genre.

Poems, Poets Poetry, by Helen Vendler: A book on how to read and write poetry; authored by one of the most celebrated poetry critics of the 20th and 21st centuries.

Poetry and Feminism, by The Poetry Foundation: A collection of traditional and contemporary poems and articles tracing the fight for equality and women's rights through poetry.

Poets on Place, by W. T. Pfefferle: An anthology documenting the importance of place in the work of sixty-two poets; features poems and interviews with poets such as Campbell McGrath, Carol Muske-Dukes, Terrance Hayes, Alberto Rios, Natasha Trethewey, Charles Wright, and many others.

Poetry Speaks: A book plus CDs that features the work of the most influential writers in modern poetry from 1892 to 1997. This book combines their most significant poems with the authors themselves reading their poetry on audio CD.

The Art of Daring, by Carl Phillips: A book of six insightful essays inspiring poets to push the boundaries of their work.

The Art of Recklessness, by Dean Young: A book of provocative essays that dares poets to move beyond the fundamentals of poetic craft and harness their recklessness.

The Art of the Poetic Line, by James Longenbach: A book that examines the function of line in metered, rhymed, syllabic, and free verse.

The Book of Forms, by Lewis Turco: A book outlining the fundamentals of traditional, odd, and invented forms of poetry.

The Gorgeous Nothings, by Emily Dickinson: A collection of the first full-color facsimile edition of Emily Dickinson's manuscripts ever to appear—exactly as she wrote it on scraps of envelopes.

The Life of Poetry, by Muriel Rukeyser: A book whereby a celebrated poet examines the ways poetry can improve the quality of life for creative individuals everywhere.

The Practicing Poet: Writing Beyond the Basics, edited by Diane Lockward: An anthology of essays on craft, including poems, prompts, and tips by over a hundred contemporary poets.

The Triggering Town, by Richard Hugo: A book advocating an approach to poetry reliant on following triggering subjects, words, rhythms, and sounds to drive the poem forward.

Troubling the Line: Trans and Genderqueer Poetry and Poetics, edited by T.C. Tolbert and Trace Peterson: A collection of poetry by transgender and genderqueer writers.

U.S. Latinx Voices in Poetry, by The Poetry Foundation: A broad and inclusive collection designed to introduce new readers to Latinx poets in the United States.

Writing Metrical Poetry, by William Baer: A book outlining how to write metrical poetry in all the major forms, from blank verse and quatrains to sonnets and villanelles.

Additional Resources

Academy of American Poets: The nation's largest membership-based nonprofit organization advocating for American poets and poetry. Its many programs and publications include Poets.org and Poem-a-Day, which is the first place of publication for new poems by 260 poets annually.

Association of Writers and Writing Programs: Provides support, advocacy, resources, and community to nearly 50,000 writers, 550 college and university creative writing programs, and 150 writers' conferences and centers. It holds the country's largest annual conference, a destination for writers, teachers, students, editors, and publishers. Each year more than 12,000 attendees join.

Berl's Poetry Shop: A carefully curated selection of only poetry from small publishers, plus reading events and workshops in Brooklyn, New York.

Canto Mundo: A national organization that cultivates a community of Latinx poets through workshops, symposia, and public reading. It seeks to provide a space for creation, documentation, and critical analysis.

Cave Canem: An organization committed to cultivating the artistic and professional growth of African American poets by offering fellowships, workshops, and programs.

Colrain Manuscript Conference: An intensive, multi-day retreat for poets with manuscripts in need of revision or feedback. The conference has regular retreats at venues in New Mexico, Massachusetts, Vermont, and Washington.

Dodge Poetry Festival: The largest poetry event in North America, representing the most eminent contemporary poets at its four-day, biennial festival.

Gotham Writers Workshop: The largest adult-education creative writing school in the U.S., offering creative writing classes as well as in-person courses in New York City.

Grolier Poetry Book Shop: The oldest continuous poetry book shop in the United States, which stocks over 15,000 current volumes of trade, small press, and university poetry publications. The store hosts regular readings, author events, book signings, and more in Cambridge, Massachusetts.

Hip-Hop Shakespeare Company: A music theatre production company aimed at exploring the social, cultural, and linguistic parallels between the works of William Shakespeare and modern-day hip-hop artists.

Lambda Literary Foundation: An LGBTQ literary organization nurturing and advocating for LGBTQ writers, including the annual Lambda Literary Awards, which identify and honor the best lesbian, gay, bisexual, and transgender books.

Poetry Off the Shelf: Poetry Foundation's podcast, which explores the diverse world of contemporary poetry; hosts readings by poets, interviews with critics, and short poetry documentaries.

Poets House Public Library: A poetry library with over 70,000 titles that is among the largest and most comprehensive independent poetry collections available to the public. *Poets House* holds events, workshops, and talks for poets in New York City.

Poetry Foundation: Publisher of *Poetry* magazine, this independent literary organization is committed to a vigorous presence for poetry in our culture. Their website contains countless educational articles, essays, and resources for poets and educators.

The Slowdown with Tracy K. Smith: Podcast of former U.S. Poet Laureate Tracy K. Smith, who selects and presents a different author's poem every weekday.

About the Authors

Christopher Salerno is the author of five books of poems and the editor of Saturnalia Books. His most recent collection is *Sun & Urn*, selected by the late Thomas Lux for the Georgia Poetry Prize. Previous books include *ATM* (Georgetown Review Prize), *Minimum Heroic* (Mississippi Review Poetry Prize), and *Whirligig*. He has also received the Two Sylvias Press Chapbook Award, the Laurel Review Chapbook Prize, and a New Jersey State Council on the Arts fellowship. Other poems can be found in the *New York Times Magazine*, *New Republic*, *American Poetry Review*, *New England Review*, and elsewhere. He is a Professor of English at William Paterson University. He can be reached at csalernopoet.com.

Kelsea Habecker is a poet, writer, teacher, retreat leader, and personal coach. Her collections of poetry include *Hollow Out*, selected by U.S. Poet Laureate Charles Simic; *The Walrus Wives*, a chapbook; and *North Wife*, forthcoming from Salmon Poetry in County Clare, Ireland. She also writes nonfiction and fiction. Kelsea teaches university writing courses and coaches clients and writers privately. She leads women's retreats in writing, creativity, self-discovery, and empowerment. She earned her master's of fine arts in poetry from Bennington College, her BA from Randolph-Macon Woman's College, and she has a post-graduate degree in education. She can be reached at kelseahabecker.com.

Printed in the USA
CPSIA information can be obtained
at www.ICGtesting.com
LVHW060433120124
768705LV00007B/38